MONSAY WHITNEY

Monsay Whitney grew up in North London and studied at local comprehensive schools. She graduated from St Mary's University in 2009 with a degree in Drama and Performance.

In 2007, she embarked on an acting career when she landed the role of Marie in *Yard Gal*, and she took up writing in 2012, after taking part in the Lyric Young Writers class.

As well as being developed and shown by and at the Lyric Hammersmith, her play *Hand to Mouth* was chosen by Simon Stephens as part of Theatre503's 'Playwright Presents' scheme.

She is Playwright Associate Artist for nabokov.

Monsay Whitney

BOX CLEVER

NICK HERN BOOKS

London

www.nickhernbooks.co.uk

A Nick Hern Book

Box Clever first published in Great Britain in 2017 as a paperback original by Nick Hern Books Limited, The Glasshouse, 49a Goldhawk Road, London W12 8QP, in association with nabokov and The Marlowe

Box Clever copyright © 2017 Monsay Whitney

Monsay Whitney has asserted her moral right to be identified as the author of this work

Front cover image: Shutterstock/Kireevl

Designed and typeset by Nick Hern Books, London
Printed in the UK by Mimeo Ltd, Huntingdon, Cambridgeshire PE29 6XX

A CIP catalogue record for this book is available from the British Library

ISBN 978 1 84842 694 8

Woodland CARBON
www.woodlandcarbon.co.uk
NICK HERN BOOKS
Printed on Carbon Captured paper

Box Clever was first produced by nabokov and The Marlowe, Canterbury, and performed in Paines Plough's Roundabout, Summerhall, as part of the Edinburgh Festival Fringe on 4 August 2017. The cast was as follows:

Monsay Whitney
Avi Simmons

Director	Stef O'Driscoll
Producer	Liz Counsell (for nabokov)
Producer	Kimberley Sanders (for The Marlowe)
Lighting Designer and Production Manager	Joe Price
Sound Designer	Dominic Kennedy
Set and Costume Designer	Lucy McGeown
Movement Director	Yassmin Foster
Assistant Director	Melanie Phillips
Clowning Consultancy	Natasha Bergg
Dramaturgy	James Baldwin (for The Marlowe)

Box Clever has been developed through The Marlowe Roar Programme and has been made possible with the support of The Marlowe Theatre Development Trust.

For Mark

Characters

MARNIE, *heavily made-up, late twenties*

JOANNE, *social worker*
LIAM, *Marnie's ex*
STEVIE, *Marnie's ex*
CHARLENE, *housemate*
FI FI, *Marnie's key worker*
EMMA, *support worker*
ESTATE AGENT
MAN IN FRONT
BUS DRIVER
GILLIAN, *Marnie's mother*
ELIJAH, *Theresa's son*
THERESA, *housemate*
VERONICA, *housemate, Damien's mother*
DANNY, *Marnie's ex, Autumn's father*
SAM, *housemate*
STEVIE'S GIRLFRIEND
AUTUMN, *Marnie's daughter*
SECURITY
RED-FACED POSH FELLA
YOUNG POLICEMAN
OLD POLICEMAN
FLORENCE, *housemate*
SYLVIA, *housing adviser*

There is no specification as to cast size.

This text went to press before the end of rehearsals and so may differ slightly from the play as performed.

*The actor – or actors – is/are present on stage during entrance
of the audience – acknowledgement, pleasantries. Then –*

MARNIE *sat, slumped, still, staring ahead, deep in thought,
chewing gum. This goes on for some time until she removes the
gum and disposes of it in paper. She replaces the old gum with
new gum. Two of them. Continues chewing.*

JOANNE. Miss McCabe? Marnie? They'll be ready for you
shortly.

MARNIE (*to* JOANNE). How long are they gonna be?

JOANNE. No more than five minutes.

MARNIE. I can't do it.

JOANNE. Well. Er. Er? We've been over this –

MARNIE. I've had a think about it and. There must be someone
who can help. *Someone's* gotta be prepared to help us. This is
a joke. I'm just not talking to the right people.

JOANNE. We're helping as much as we can.

MARNIE. This ain't help! This ain't *helping us*.

JOANNE. I know it's frustrating, when we don't get what we
want –

MARNIE. We haven't done anything wrong!

JOANNE. Nobody's saying you have –

MARNIE. You're not listening to me.

JOANNE. But it will be better for you if –

MARNIE. What was I s'posed to do?

JOANNE. For both of you, if –

MARNIE. Keep my mouth shut? Bumble along like I don't
know nothing?

JOANNE. Calm down.

MARNIE. Like you have? Like everyone else has?

JOANNE. The alternative is –

MARNIE. Yes I know the fucking alternative! I'm not fucking thick!

JOANNE. Stop. Just. Stop.

MARNIE. You've failed her. You've failed that little girl. Twice.

JOANNE. So you keep saying.

MARNIE. I'm not doing it.

JOANNE. We're going round in circles again.

MARNIE. I'm not doing it. I'm not doing it. I'm not doing it.

Lights fade.

Lights come up – MARNIE's *in her bedroom. She has a dressing gown over her clothes.*

(*To audience.*) September the 8th.

AUDIO. *You have twenty. Seven. New messages. First message received on. September. Second. At two. Fifty. Seven. A.M.*

LIAM. It's Liam. Pick up the phone. Where are you?

Silence.

I know where you are anyway.

MARNIE. Goron then, where am I?

LIAM. Hammersmith, probably. Staying with Connie.

MARNIE. Ha! I think. I'm closer than you think, ya cunt.

LIAM. I'm not gonna chase you. Look, Marnie, I need a favour.

MARNIE. I call them The Three Musketeers.

LIAM. I need a bath, Marnie. I ain't had a bath since you left.

MARNIE. Let me draw you a picture: first there was Danny.
I'm eighteen. I'm a bit of a needy div. In fact, so needy, is
the eighteen-year-old me, that I'm actually under a
psychiatrist for it. And the psychiatrist's got me pumped up
on these antipsychotics they call Olanzapine – what make
you well fat. I mean, in hindsight, Danny must be pretty
fucked up himself, to go out with me in the first place. We
split up. We get back together. I have a kid with him later on
down the line. Which makes him fucking impossible to get
rid of nowadays. Not that he's ever been a father to her. And
that's about all Danny contributes to this story.

AUDIO. *Nine. Thirty. Six. A.M.*

LIAM. It's me again. Is this it then? You're gone?

MARNIE. Then there was *Liam*. I find him in a squat party on
the Arden Estate. I'm twenty now. I'm still fucking baffed
about life, but I've brushed up on the art of seduction. Here
we are, sitting on a wall, waiting for his bus, the morning
after the night we met. I've got one eye up here and one eye
down there, buzzing off of six-and-a-half White Doves, and
he gives me the most stunning sapphire-and-diamond, white-
gold eternity ring you've ever seen. I mean it just blows me
away. He took it back a couple months later, cos it actually
was a family heirloom, belonging to his nan and that. And
she clocked it was missing.

Liam's banged up till Christmas. He's home a couple of
months and he leaves me for a bird he was in care with. Amy,
her name is. He's to-ing and fro-ing back and forth between us
for a bit. Course, Amy's gone and got herself up the duff by
him. I've ended up in a nuthouse over it. Liam says he can't be
with someone mental. Which is, you know, nice of the cunt.

It's at this point the winner in me comes out fighting. This
shit's gone on almost two years. Well no fucking more. I have
a bright idea. I reckon I'm gonna just sniff coke till I die.
I give it my best shot. Didn't die, sadly. I ain't that fucking
lucky. Did manage to balls up almost every aspect of my life
though, which is, you know, a skill in itself.

Maybe I should get some help. Or kill myself. Or go on holiday.

AUDIO. *Ten. Seventeen. A.M.*

LIAM. Why you ignoring my calls for? Answer the fucking phone, you slag.

MARNIE. And *then*, like an angel through my window, there was Stevie. I'm twenty-two. And this is it. This time. The real deal. I sit myself down and have a word with myself; Marnie, do *not* fuck this up. Don't fuck it up. I'm not good at taking direction so I talk to myself twice to ram it home.

There's this gaff in Stepney called 'The Fridge'. They call it the fridge cos it's fucking chilly in there. It's basically just a hall. With chairs in. Where they hold meetings and everyone sits around eating biscuits, talking about how much they love drugs but how they can't take them no more. We call it recovery. Anyway, I'm there because I'm like a raving fucking cokehead who keeps tryna do herself in. And Stevie's there because he's just got out of prison and he's had a pipe with his uncle after eighteen months off the white and ended up on his mum's doorstep crying out for his dad, who died of a brain tumour when he was fourteen. And he knows if he don't change real quick he's going straight back in the shovel. He makes me a cup of tea. And he smiles at me. I feel double lovely. And I just know this is gonna be something special.

Then he makes the old boot next to me a cup of tea. And he smiles at her. Slag.

I ask him where he's from. He says:

STEVIE. Bermondsey.

MARNIE. It's like this, right. When they founded London, evolution was still proper backward. They didn't know about flood banks and the river used to flood South of the Thames. So what they did, was, they stuck all the prisons and all the mental hospitals and anyone they weren't keen on, down there, in all that slush, with the hunchback rats, and basically just left them to it. Society, as it was at the time, meant that, like kids would leave home, marry someone local and move round the corner from their families. So naturally, over time, the prisoners and the mental patients procreated. Then their children procreated with one another. And so on and so forth. Have you ever looked into the eyes of someone from South East London? Normal people don't just develop the mental attributes and criminal capacity that make up a South Londoner. That shit's intrinsically bred. Stevie ain't wrapped too tight.

LIAM. Hello?

MARNIE (*to* LIAM). Liam?

LIAM. Have you listened to my voicemails?

MARNIE. Yeah.

LIAM. So? Are you anywhere near Hackney?

MARNIE (*to audience*). I tell you one thing about this geezer. He's got some fucking nerve.

LIAM. Are you close?

MARNIE. He says.

LIAM. Not close, close. But could you drive here? I've been on a mad one. I need a bath, Marnie. So can you do that for me? You don't have to come home. Just give me the keys.

MARNIE (*to* LIAM). We can't bath in our own home.

LIAM. Can you give me the keys or what?

MARNIE. No.

LIAM. You see how you are? Fuck ya then, I'll bath at Amy's. Pig tits.

MARNIE (*to audience*). Ever had the feeling you're going round in one big circle? It's like I can't stop recycling my ex-boyfriends.

LIAM. And another thing – you think you're so smart, running away, don't ya. Embarrassing me. See when I see you again, you're gonna wish you hadn't bothered. Filthy, dirty grass.

MARNIE (*to audience*). Ten years back and forth between a trio of arseholes and nothing to show for it except a baby, an Argos ring and a beat-up nose. Well I don't wanna live like that no more. Course a lot of women would of chose a round-the-world trip. I mean that's ideal really. If you're looking to go off in search of yourself. But um, well to cut to the chase, I fled to Merrygold House.

CHARLENE. What d'you want it to say?

MARNIE. Charlene's in the doorway. Next door, room five.

(*To* CHARLENE.) Just like, 'Please can you stop giving me tickets, I'm out of petrol, I can't move it. It's nearly Christmas!' Or is that stronging it?

CHARLENE. *It's September.*

MARNIE (*to audience*). Charlene scrolls, brow furrowed in concentration. When she's done she hands the paper to me, two-inch letters, red crayon.

CHARLENE. To ticket warden.

This vehicle has broken down and we are seeking recovery so stop putting ras-clot tickets on n go home and res ya bumba foot.

Driver.

MARNIE. Charlene sashays downstairs and out the front door, sticks the letter on my windscreen, and struts off to college.

MARNIE *sneaks a cigarette.*

I found a johnny in the drawer, when I got here. Sort of unexpected, given the circumstance – but useful, nonetheless. I stretched it over the smoke alarm.

Mostly, I nose at the window. Inspect the cars. Wonder if he's spotted my motor. Bog at the garden and that.

Florence – upstairs, room eight – is adding liquid combust to a smouldering settee at the minute. Not the full ticket, Florence. Don't make it fair though. I mean if your average mental defective dragged a donated couch out the living room and into the yard to set fire to for the hell of it, the office'd get the right arsehole. If it was, say, *me – I'd* be up in the dock, Monday morning. You can't say to Florence, 'You're allowed to torch the couch,' after you've said to me:

FI FI. That's the second window you've 'accidentally' put your foot through, Marnie, if you do it again we'll have a look at evicting you.

MARNIE. Where's the consistency? See, there. The office blinds just twitched.

(*To* FI FI.) Are you gonna leave that office, Fi Fi? (*To audience*.) I say.

(*To* FI FI.) Fi Fi? Can you hear me or what? Are you gonna have her up for that or no?

(*To audience*.) Like fuck she is. Who's gonna confront Florence? Not me, mate. She must be six-two.

Sound effects – door knocks.

FI FI. Marnie.

MARNIE (*to* FI FI). I'm a bit busy.

FI FI. I can't hear you.

MARNIE. I said I'm sleeping.

FI FI. I need to speak to you.

MARNIE. Oh for fuck's sake.

(*To audience*.) It's difficult to describe Fi Fi without ripping her to bits. I can't be arsed to go into it. I give her the benefit of the doubt for the first couple weeks. Had a go at liking her and that. Only then I come to my senses. Realised, didn't I. I can't be expected to go round giving preferential treatment to every woman who declares herself a feminist. Marching against the pay gap don't exempt you from being a cunt. So you see I could sense from the start. That it'd be best all round if we steered clear of each other. But then she assigned herself to be my key worker. Which basically gives her licence to follow me round, sucking the life out of me. She's like a roving mosquito handpicking an arse cheek. Any arse'd do, probably. But it's personal when it's your own.

I leave Fi Fi to continue her morning rounds and slip down stairs into the office. Emma's at the computer. Emma does the late shift. She's lovely, Emma. Different breed from Fi Fi.

EMMA. Sorry, sweetheart, am I in the way?

MARNIE. Log-in to the home-swapper website, read through my advertisement, hoping for a miracle. I've been stuck here for three months. Honestly, I thought I'd be gone by now. There's really only three options left. Okay so, one: stay put and hope to God I can find an online swap; two: give my flat up and go homeless, let the council ship me out to some isolated village, where the folk have eleven fingers and there's only two buses a day; or three: wait for Liam to get lifted by the Old Bill and go back home. I mean I can't exactly go back for good. I know that. He will get out at some point but it would give me some time to search for an exchange from the comfort of my own gaff.

ESTATE AGENT. Large, two-bedroom, corner house for exchange –

MARNIE. My advert reads.

ESTATE AGENT. A solid family home, with a medium-sized front garden, which is paved and could be used as a driveway, and a large, very tranquil back garden which is grass, and trees and beautiful plants –

MARNIE. And all that malarky. I say that it's –

ESTATE AGENT. Tucked away on a nice little road, that's very quiet, never had no trouble –

MARNIE. And I explain that it's –

ESTATE AGENT. – on top of bus routes X, Y and Z and a train line leading into the city.

MARNIE. I write that –

ESTATE AGENT. It needs a good lick of paint –

MARNIE. So as not to waste no one's time. In the 'What are you looking for?' section, I say –

ESTATE AGENT. I'm looking for a two-bedroom like-for-like property, in London, I'm not considering anywhere further afield because my daughter's starting school.

MARNIE. And right at the bottom of the paragraph, I write:

ESTATE AGENT. This is my mum's house, we're searching for a three-way swap.

MARNIE. Quick scan through my replies. I'm losing the will to live.

September the 11th. No petrol. Can you believe I've give up my job for this shit? Between a rock and a fucking hard place. My kid's five miles away, waiting for me to take her to school. It's her first fucking day. I've been stuck at the train station for fifteen minutes behind a fella who's got a fucking question for everything.

MAN IN FRONT. Sorry, are you waiting?

MARNIE (*to* MAN IN FRONT). Nah, mate. Just stood here admiring the decor, whilst contemplating the meaning of life.

(*To audience*.) Matey starts counting out his coppers into ten-pee piles… I make a run for the peasant wagon.

BUS DRIVER. Can passengers move down the bus please.

MARNIE. D'you know, I've *never* known any bus to hum of piss to the extent of the 279.

The scruff cunt next to me scratches his smelly balls and indiscreetly sniffs his fingers. Our eyes meet. He chucks me an algae-coated grin. I can't work it out. That's actual fucking plants growing in between his teeth. I pick up a paper and bury my head in its centre pages. Boris Johnson says that the biggest Cornflakes tend to end up at the top of the packet. Well I say the biggest Cornflakes were at the top of the packet to begin with and the Cornflakes at the bottom

got knocked about and crushed and shit. Why the fuck are
we talking about Cornflakes, anyway? It's too early for this
bollocks. I need a beer. I *need* a beer – but I settle for a
coffee – my mum's a cranky bitch at the best of times.

Gillian opens the door, child on her hip.

GILLIAN. Do you know this woman, Autumn?

MARNIE. She says.

GILLIAN. She claims to be your mother.

MARNIE. Round of applause for my mum.

Sound effects – applause.

That's a sarcastic round of applause. I don't find her in the
least bit funny. Step inside.

(*To* GILLIAN.) Anyways – (*To audience.*) I say – (*To*
GILLIAN.) has he been here?

GILLIAN. Who?

MARNIE. You know who – Liam.

GILLIAN. Nope –

MARNIE (*to audience*). She goes.

GILLIAN. Nope.

MARNIE (*to* GILLIAN). Are you lying? (*To audience.*) I say –
(*To* GILLIAN.) you better not be lying to me.

(*To audience.*) Gillian eyeballs me.

GILLIAN. I AM NOT A LIAR –

MARNIE. *She is a fucking liar.*

(*To* GILLIAN.) Well it wouldn't be the first time, would it –
(*To audience.*) I say. Oh here she goes:

GILLIAN. And if he did come round here, ever again –

MARNIE. Grabs arm, pinches –

GILLIAN. Which I doubt, because I've asked him not to – and
he respects what I say, unlike some – if he did come round

here, I WOULDN'T FUCKING LET HIM IN, because I'm
not allowed to have my own friends, am I.

MARNIE. I fantasise about snapping her scrawny arm as she
shoves me back out the door.

(*To* GILLIAN.) You're really fucking selfish!!! (*To
audience*.) I scream. The door slams in my face. (*To*
GILLIAN.) GILLIAN!!!

(*To audience*.) Back on the 279, the kid in tow.

AUTUMN. Can we play I Spy?

MARNIE. My head's tuned in to Shit FM:

*Sound effects – speech punctuated by static/the tuning of
a radio:*

Are they…? Are they actually fucking shagging or
something? Seriously. Is my mum banging Liam? I mean
what is it with them two, he's not even her fucking son.

It's a bit mental, but it's funny, right, because one half of my
brain manufactures bullshit. And the the other half buys it.

*Sound effects – speech punctuated by static/the tuning of
a radio:*

No way, man. She's in her fifties. And you're her daughter,
for crying out loud! Then again – I wouldn't put it past *him* –
and she ain't had it in a while…

Ten past six. School run done. Undo the Chub. Twist my key
in the Yale. Bolts are on. I thump on the window for
assistance. I can't work out if they're tryna keep them out, or
us in. I'm either completely on the ball with this or paranoid
as fuck, I've been smoking weed with Alex – downstairs,
room one. At night. To help me fall asleep. Alex is from
Peckham. She's got the eyes. Up the swanny again I reckon.
She looks about five months gone. Ain't gonna admit it
though. Not in here. She'd have Social Services crawling all
over her. I like Alex. She's got a good heart.

Emma answers the door.

EMMA. Fi Fi wants to talk to you, Marnie.

MARNIE. Drag my shop up the stairs; basics, courtesy of the food bank, park my arse at the kitchen table and peanut-butter my roll. Veronica shuffles up next to me. Two along, room six. Eyes like pickled onions. I can't have her. The office is all like:

FI FI. Veronica's a churchgoer. Veronica's got a degree. How many tongues can we stick up Veronica's batty-hole at the same time.

MARNIE. It transpires that in the eight hours' reprieve I've had from this hellhole, Veronica's oddball son has beat up Elijah –

ELIJAH. Mum!

MARNIE. – on the top floor, and banged out his front tooth. Elijah's five, six years younger than Damien, and his mum, Theresa – upstairs room nine – is understandably fucking fuming. (Damien's not his actual name, but I'm bound by confidentiality and I reckon 'Damien' draws pretty apt connotations.)

Here's the thing. Veronica's got her head so far up this little wanker's arse, she can't see the wood for the trees. Any normal mother would apologise to all the kids he's been let loose to batter and pull his arse into line. Not Veronica, she goes down to the office to put in another complaint that she's being bullied. Fi Fi pulls Theresa in. Points her to sit opposite Veronica. Reprimands her for swearing. Whereupon Veronica threatens to kick Theresa's feet from under her.

THERESA. Go for it –

MARNIE. Says Theresa –

THERESA. I've been waiting for the chance to knock your face off that turkey neck and shove it up your born-again arse.

MARNIE. And a tear-up escalates quickly from then.

Fi Fi's straight on the phone to the police.

So here we are. Sat round the kitchen table. Veronica badgering me to pick sides.

VERONICA. You've changed since she came here.

MARNIE. Goes Veronica. She's only fucking crying.

VERONICA. We used to be close. I thought you was a nice person, Marnie.

MARNIE. She's only known me five weeks, the disordered bitch.

What makes you think I'm a nice person? I think.

I'm an arsehole.

Veronica ain't getting a rise out of me, so she fucks off in a huff. Oh no, she's back again. Oh, she's crying. God she's sobbing out loud and hyperventilating with a dead plant in her hands. I'm eating off the table when she shoves the dead plant under my nose. It's pretty obvious Theresa's responsible for ripping her plant out its pot by the root, but come on, this is the third time it's been attacked now –

(*To* VERONICA.) Stop leaving it in the fucking garden?

VERONICA. Who would do something so evil? It's innocent. What did it do to deserve this? Do you see? Do you see how your friend is? Oh my Lord, she's evil.

MARNIE (*to audience*). She's snotting and shit. There's a great dollop of spit on her bottom lip. I hate that. Wonder if a touch of small talk'll ease the situation?

(*To* VERONICA.) Can't it re-root itself?

(*To audience*.) My input only intensifies Veronica's grief.

VERONICA. No! It's dead!

MARNIE. She screams.

VERONICA. IT'S DEAD!

MARNIE. Fuck me. It's a plant, mate. I don't think it felt anything when it passed.

SAM. Marnie, get the door.

MARNIE (*to* SAM). You got legs, ain't ya?

SAM. So.

MARNIE (*to audience*). So? says Sam – the moody bitch.

(*To* SAM.) So you're downstairs!

SAM. Get the fucking door.

MARNIE. No.

(*To audience.*) Sam's the new girl, she's moved into room eight. Fi Fi sent Florence packing – the settee episode turned out to be the final straw. I can't get Florence off my phone now. She rings me six times a day to chat about her hostel. Don't think she's got no friends. Saying that, neither have I. Sam's from Surrey or Portsmouth or somewhere far like that. Sam's got an eyebrow piercing and seaside tattoos. I imagine that in Surrey or Portsmouth or wherever the fuck Sam's from, she's got a rep for being the town bully, cos she stamps about here like she runs the gaff. Big chip on her shoulder. Sam says Londoners are all up theirselves. Her every waking moment's been spent banging on about how Surrey or Portsmouth or wherever the fuck she's from is underrated and how London ain't all it's cracked up to be. And I'm like –

(*To* SAM.) Well if it's so fucking great in Surrey –

SAM. Portsmouth.

MARNIE. Same thing. Why don't the Queen wanna live there?

(*To audience.*) I ain't getting the fucking door. Think I'll go back to bed and rot some more.

Hello?

DANNY. I wanna see my kid.

MARNIE (*to* DANNY). Have a look, it's Danny, car thief turned arms dealer.

DANNY. Shut up.

MARNIE. Long time, Dan, wondered how long it'd take you to remember your daughter.

DANNY. Why ain't you replying to my letters?

MARNIE. Danny, this ain't really a good time, mate.

DANNY. I sent you a visiting order.

MARNIE. Do yourself a favour, Dan –

DANNY. I've got fucking rights!

MARNIE. Don't try and come at me with the concerned-father act.

DANNY. Marnie!

MARNIE. Dan, I'm going.

DANNY. Marnie!

MARNIE. I'm going, I'm going, I'll speak to you another time.

(*To audience*.) I was awake till half-four this morning.
Pondering what Stevie was up to. Probably sleeping, given
it was half-four, but you can never second-guess the prick.
I ain't had enough to worry about lately, so my head thought
it'd give me some more to contemplate.

*Sound effects – speech punctuated by static/the tuning of
a radio.*

We sat in the dark, just me and my head, jumping at noises
we didn't hear, considering survival strategies for if Liam
come through the bedroom door with a carving knife.

Realistically, my head's probably more dangerous than any
fucker out there.

Back to Stevie. I can't stop obsessing about him. I wonder if
this means I miss him? I think it must. Which pisses me off.
Then again. Stevie actually ain't all that bad. When you
compare him to Liam. I mean, he never beat me up. But then
he did give me chlamydia. Maybe I should give him another
chance. I just want someone to love me for the horrific,
raging, emotionally unpredictable bitch that I am.

Sound effects – door knocks.

FI FI. Marnie? Did Emma speak to you?

MARNIE (*to* FI FI). I'll pay it tomorrow.

FI FI. It's not about your rent.

MARNIE. I'm a bit busy, Fi Fi.

FI FI. We've had the police on the phone.

MARNIE. I didn't see nothing. Have they bailed her?

FI FI. It's not to do with Theresa.

MARNIE. What's it to do with then?

FI FI. You, Marnie.

MARNIE. Me?

Sound effects – heart pounding.

FI FI. Can you open the door?

MARNIE. What do they wanna speak to *me* about?

FI FI. Harassment.

MARNIE. Harassment?

FI FI. Harassment charges.

MARNIE. Harassment charges?

FI FI. Do you know a Stephen Gallagher?

MARNIE (*to audience*). What a cunt.

Here's the deal: Stevie was getting hold of yet another bird behind my back and it's all come out in the wash. In my absence they've got together and in a bid to make her jealous, he's told her I desperately want him back. And that that's why I ring him all the time. Which ain't true. It's him begging me to come back. I only really ring him because I'm bored and I want an argument. So there's a set-to between me and this divvy bird of his. We're back and forth on the phones, Stevie claiming to love me, me texting him to fuck off. He goes back to her and says – *whatever it is he says to her* – which leads to verbals between the pair of us and a torrent of abuse, but I mean, it's standard, two-way abuse. We're giving as good as we get. Next thing, she's on the phone, screaming that he's her boyfriend –

STEVIE'S GIRLFRIEND. Fuck off, mental bitch!!!

MARNIE. Saying all this really out-of-order stuff, you know, dragging my kid into the mix. I assume, as you do, that the gloves are off. (*To* STEVIE'S GIRLFRIEND.) I'm sorry – (*To audience.*) I text her – (*To* STEVIE'S GIRLFRIEND.) I just can't take nothing you say for serious because you look like a fucking geezer and you're so thick that you don't even clock Stevie rings me as soon as you leave his flat.

(*To audience.*) So we're in the middle of one of our to-do's and she tells me that if I ever go to Selco's I'm gonna get beat up. I get to thinking about that, it's a liberty that, really. I can go where I want. So I do a bit of CSI work, you know, try and work out what Selco's I can't go to. Her Facebook profile's a touch misleading, I wasted time ringing Wimbledon, Croydon, Catford and Charlton, all to no avail. But it turns out she works in Walthamstow. True to my word, I train it up there, call her bluff.

But her manager's waiting for me when I get there and he rings the Old Bill. Proper set-up.

FI FI. Stephen Gallagher is the perpetrator, isn't he, Marnie? Isn't he.

MARNIE *exhales deeply.*

MARNIE. Now admittedly there's an opportunity here, to do the honourable thing and clear Stevie's name. But in order to tell the truth, I'd have to give Liam's name up. So I decide against it. And I reckon my reasons are valid. This is my thinking: So, one: I didn't involve Stevie, he involved himself. Two: opening my big mouth don't serve much of a purpose, cos Fi Fi's already convinced herself she's on to the truth. And three: I don't think I deserve the battering I'll get if Liam finds out.

FI FI. Marnie, have you still got all the texts Stephen's been sending you?

MARNIE (*to* FI FI). No, you railroaded me into deleting everything, remember? In order to prove to you I'm serious. Fresh start, you said.

FI FI. Yeah. About that…

MARNIE. What you saying?

FI FI. If you could just open the door? Marnie?

MARNIE. Are you saying you've made me delete a phone full of evidence, Fi Fi?

FI FI. Can you open the door for me? Marnie, open the door, love. Open the damn door!!!!

MARNIE (*to audience*). September the 15th. So it turns out, cos Stevie's had the brass nerve to ring me pleading his innocence –

STEVIE. Why you being like that, Marnie?

MARNIE. That not only has this bird filed a false allegation of harassment against me, she's managed to coax Stevie into doing the same. What a piss-take. I never had that level of control over him and believe me, that ain't for a lack of trying.

All this caper from the girlfriend's backfired on Stevie though, cos she's unwittingly implicated him in a domestic-violence case. Fi Fi's coming down hard on me to press charges against him. She just won't let the subject drop. Says the only way I'm gonna get off with this harassment thingy is if I make a counter-allegation. Reckons she'll destroy his life.

FI FI. He'll wish he was never born. Believe me. I know how to speak to the police –

MARNIE. She says.

FI FI. I'll have them eating out of the palm of my hand.

MARNIE. Which amuses me a little bit but terrifies me more. I mean I'm worried about getting on the wrong side of the woman. I ain't sure what level of ruthless vindictiveness I'm dealing with here.

I decide I'm gonna have to put Stevie to bed. Here and now. Once and for all. Fi Fi's managed to complicate matters enough – I can't, *I can't* have Social Services sticking their oar in.

Log back in to home-swapper. It strikes me that I might never find an exchange. Charlene's got a two-bed in Leytonstone, it's a shame we all just can't swap between us.

I'm about to give another home-swapper a volley of abuse when I chuck up across the computer screen and have to leg it back upstairs to the shitter. It's this house. This house is making me sick.

Sound effect – door opening.

FI FI. Living room. House meeting.

MARNIE. There's a house meeting every Friday at half-four, where Fi Fi addresses all the issues we reached agreements on last week, that no one's stuck to since. Nothing's ever resolved. But Fi Fi has a breakdown if I don't show up. First up this evening: unpaid rent. It's starting to look like I'm the only tenant who actually pays to stay here. Next: room swaps. This is an ongoing argument between Veronica, Sam and Alex over who's got the biggest room and who's the most deserving of it – which is none of 'em– basically, cos they're all in fucking rent arrears. My room's poky but it's the only room what ain't got rats. Dirty kitchens. Dirty bathrooms. Housemates who don't partake in the weekly chore, which is everyone – and kids. Or more precisely, *my* kid. We're holding a house meeting. *About my kid.*

FI FI. Autumn isn't staying here. We've already discussed this, Marnie. She should be in a place of safety.

MARNIE (*to* FI FI). She's safe at my mum's though.

FI FI. You can't just leave her at your mother's house.

MARNIE. You go on about this like she's been abandoned. She's staying at her nan's. It's a private arrangement.

FI FI. She should be socialising with the other children.

MARNIE. Well I'd rather she didn't. Not being horrible, but she's quite together.

FI FI. You'll still have plenty of free time. She can attend the playscheme.

MARNIE. You're missing the point. She don't like it here. It's distressing for her.

FI FI. God, Marnie, why do you have to be so difficult? I give up with you. I give up. You can discuss Autumn's whereabouts with the family support worker.

MARNIE (*to audience*). There's a family support worker here. She's basically some sort of social worker. Which is a bit of drama for a couple of the mums. But not me. My reports are gleaming.

(*To* FI FI.) Fine.

FI FI. Right then.

MARNIE. I'll think about it.

FI FI. No, Marnie, you've had long enough to think about it. Either Autumn resides here, permanently or –

FI FI *gives an over-dramatic, frustrated exhale.*

There are thirteen women in this house. Ten children, a baby expected in the next two weeks and a long line of mothers who will happily take your room – you only have to look at the statistics. You're wasting resources.

MARNIE. *I'm* wasting your resources?

FI FI. One last thing –

MARNIE (*to audience*). She says and she scrolls down her list.

(*To* FI FI.) Hang on a minute – *I'm* a waste of your resources?

FI FI. Somebody's been letting the black-and-white cat in the house.

MARNIE (*to audience*). They all look at me.

(*To* FI FI.) What cat?

FI FI. We have a witness who saw you locking the stray in the house, Marnie.

MARNIE (*to audience*). I turn to Veronica and give her the look.

(*To* FI FI.) Not me, mate.

FI FI. We have a zero-tolerance policy on animals.

MARNIE. Zero tolerance? The gaffs riddled with animals –
we're alive with vermin, in case you haven't noticed.

FI FI. And another thing. Somebody poured half a bottle of
bleach down the side of the oven – the children found a
dying mouse on the kitchen floor.

MARNIE. What d'you expect me to do? Live alongside the rats?

FI FI. They're not rats. They're not. They're mice.

MARNIE. You don't have to live with them! You're alright.
You can go home!

FI FI. You're blowing this all out of proportion, Marnie!
They're not that big!

MARNIE. Not that big???? They're bowling round like they're
on fucking steroids –

VERONICA. You know in some parts of the world mice are
considered sacred? Anyway, I think they're cute.

MARNIE (to VERONICA). Oh fuck off.

VERONICA. I wish they would leave my apples alone though.

MARNIE. You're still leaving your fruit out?

VERONICA. I should be able to leave my fruit where I want,
Marnie! This is our home. We have human rights.

MARNIE (to FI FI). See what I mean – they're backward, I'm
sorry, they're weird, Fi Fi. Are they for real? Can you hear
that? They think the rats are cute… they're feeding the
fucking rats! I've got a phobia.

FI FI. Just leave the mice alone, from now on.

MARNIE. I ain't bothering the rats. I don't go looking for
rats. I'm just saying. They can't live here. They can't. It's
disgusting. It's me or the rats. It's me or the rats, Fi Fi. Why do
we even need to have this conversation? Eurgh. How about
you stick the rats in your statistics? Better still, stick the rats

up your fucking arse. I mean it ain't normal, really, is it? No one here's normal. *Where are all the normal people????!*

(*To audience*.) We sit in silence for an awkwardly long time while I wait for this meeting to be over. I can feel twelve sets of eyes burning into my cheeks.

Fi Fi reads us out a Maya Angelou poem, and I observe the performance of it all. I wonder if Maya Angelou ever imagined her words might be kidnapped and murdered out loud by this hideously patronising, never-quite-genuine, pseudo-feminist. When she's done reading the poem, she launches into a speech about who Maya Angelou is, as if to reach out to us thick and theory-less failures of feminism. Two minutes in it feels like this could go on for ever until Charlene pipes up:

CHARLENE. Yeah we all know who Maya Angelou is, Fi Fi.

FI FI. Really?

MARNIE. Fi Fi's stunned to hear that we support women's rights.

THERESA. We did go to school –

MARNIE. Says Theresa.

THERESA. We ain't ignorant.

MARNIE. And with that, Fi Fi picks up her purse bag, hands over to Emma, and trots off on a romantic weekend with her fella. A well-earned break. For me I mean, not him.

I make my way to Gillian's house. Thinking. Thinking. You know I'm not sure if I'm going through a nervous breakdown already, or whether I'm just heading for one. Drag the recycling bin over to the garden fence, hop up on it, lean over the gate, lift the latch, let myself in through the back door. Help myself to bread and jam. Kick my shoes off. Venture upstairs. Two steps at a time, spot… Liam's trainer… laying on its side. Stop, seize up, you know like, paralysed. Continue up to the landing, creeping now… Liam's jacket… on a coat hanger over the airing cupboard. Wrap my palm around the door knob, ready to catch them in the act. Burst through Gillian's bedroom door.

GILLIAN. Jesus, Marnie! Can't you use the doorbell like everyone else?

MARNIE. But there's no Liam. Gillian's folding her washing.

(*To* GILLIAN.) Where's Autumn?

GILLIAN. In the back bedroom, napping.

MARNIE. Are you fucking him?

GILLIAN. Don't be so disgusting!

MARNIE. Are you? Is that what this is?

GILLIAN. No!

MARNIE. Then why are you doing this to me? Why? You're s'posed to be my fucking mother!

GILLIAN. He's sleeping on park benches!

MARNIE. Why do you fucking care?

GILLIAN. Well it's put me in a difficult position, all this, hasn't it.

MARNIE. Not really!

GILLIAN. What am I supposed to say to him then?

MARNIE. Tell him to fuck off! Tell him he's made his fucking bed! That he's crossed a line! I dunno! Summink!

GILLIAN. And then you two make up and I'm what? The bad guy again.

MARNIE. As if I'm gonna get back with him. You don't give me no credit!

GILLIAN. Marnie –

MARNIE. Don't fucking touch me, don't touch me, Gillian! Are you really this thick? I could lose my kid over this!

GILLIAN. Oh well, he's not going to harm Autumn, is he. For Christ's sake.

MARNIE. Nah, just me! I mean what do I matter?

(*To audience*.) I pick up an ornamental iron and crack myself over the head with it for effect.

MARNIE's *head starts pissing blood*.

(*To* GILLIAN – *crying*.) What did I ever do to you? Ay? Do you really hate me this much? Is that how little you think of me? I'm fucking done with you. I'm so fucking done with you, Gillian.

GILLIAN. You're bleeding.

MARNIE. What? Oh for fuck's sake, how've I done that?

GILLIAN. You hit yourself in the head.

MARNIE. Yes I'm aware of that, thank you. I weren't s'posed to properly cave it in.

(*To audience*.) Wrap a towel round my head, ring a cab, cart Autumn up to the hospital to get my head glued back together. We've been sitting here for fucking hours. While I bleed to death.

AUTUMN. Can we play a game?

MARNIE (*to* AUTUMN). Not right now, Autumn.

(*To audience*.) September the 16th. Nine o'clock, fingers prodding my face, wake up, it's blurry. I can hear the kitchen bustling.

AUTUMN. Mum –

MARNIE (*to audience*). Says Autumn,

AUTUMN. Can you play with me?

MARNIE (*to* AUTUMN). Not now, Autumn.

AUTUMN. Mum, I hungry.

MARNIE (*to audience*). Roll on my side, prop up on an elbow, everything hurts.

(*To* AUTUMN.) I'm not well – (*To audience*.) I say – (*To* AUTUMN.) can you get the cereal from the kitchen? Ask Alex to get it down? And I'll pour it in here.

(*To audience*.) Doze off. The door kicks open and my eyes spring to.

AUTUMN. Mouse. Mouse.

MARNIE. Throw myself up expecting to gather momentum, hang limp over the bed.

AUTUMN. Mouse in box. Mummy. Mousey.

MARNIE. Look to the cereal box, look to Autumn.

(*To* AUTUMN.) Yeah, it's a toy – (*To audience*.) I say – (*To* AUTUMN.) a figurine.

AUTUMN. No, mouse.

MARNIE. No it's plastic, it's, look at the picture on the box, it's a toy.

(*To audience*.) We debate back and forth about whether or not the toy's real, until Autumn fetches it over and I stick my hand in… fish around… pull my arm out, squash the sides so I can see inside and –

Sound effect – screaming.

(*To housemates*.) Get it out!! Get it fucking out, get it out. Get it out of my room, someone help us, help, help me get it out!!!!!

(*To audience*.) The door swings open, Charlene in the doorway. The rat stands transfixed, weighing her up. Then it saunters across her foot – all brazen – and potters back towards the kitchen.

CHARLENE. You don't look good –

MARNIE. Says Charlene.

CHARLENE. Want me to bring you some chicken soup? Okay, rest up. I'll be a couple of hours.

MARNIE. Lie back down, Autumn plants herself at the end of the bed, hunts amongst the ruffled duvet for her pens, starts colouring.

AUTUMN. Do you want to colour with me?

MARNIE. And I'm dying. I'm dying. I am fucking dying.

> Half-wake up, I dunno how long later, call out to Autumn, eyes closed, check she ain't gone nowhere. She's still colouring. Squint, can half-make out Veronica in the doorway.

VERONICA. Are you sure you don't need anything?

MARNIE. Actually sort of grateful to see her there. I must drift back off for a few hours then, cos when I come to the room's in darkness. The mattress is wet through, I reckon I might of pissed myself, but then I touch the nape of my neck, my hair, drenched and sticking to my skin, realise I've run a fever. Panic sets in, I call out to Autumn, no response, call again, frantic, keep calling, keep calling, I'm losing my voice. Struggle to stand, stumble and bump across the room, smack my knee on the bed-frame, send a soup bowl flying, open the door, call down the stairs, freeze. Call again. Scream her name. Wait. Wait. And breathe a sigh of relief. I can hear Autumn's voice along the corridor. Up the stairs she shoots, Veronica on her tail, Damien trailing. (*To* AUTUMN.) Where've you been?

VERONICA. She's been playing with the other children. It was no fun for her in there.

MARNIE (*to audience*). Lock my door, stretch the sheet back over the bed, Autumn jumps in. Lie down and – this is how rough I feel – I say a prayer – like a literal prayer – to actual God. Lay in the darkness, listening out for rats. Think to myself. Even though Veronica's a creepy sorta Jesus freak and it's questionable how inappropriately affectionate Sam is towards her sons. Even though no bastard thinks it appropriate to call in Rentokil. Even though I have to run all my parental decisions by a woman with zero life experience and no kids. I'm relieved. It is a relief.

Sound effect – door knocks.

(*To* VERONICA.) Who is it?

(*To audience.*) It's Veronica.

(*To* VERONICA.) Veronica, it's two o'clock in the morning.

VERONICA *crying uncontrollably.*

Veronica, I ain't doing this again. I don't hate you... Cos you don't make no sense when you do this... Every other night, Veronica. VERONICA, FUCK OFF!!!

(*To audience*.) September the 18th. Monday afternoon. Still in bed. Fi Fi's milling about, knocking doors. She pokes her head round mine to have a moan when she clocks me:

FI FI. Jesus, Marnie, how long have you been like this? Didn't anybody think to call an ambulance? Get dressed –

MARNIE. She says.

FI FI. You're going to the hospital.

MARNIE. Back in A&E, a nurse sticks me on intravenous fluids and tells me I'm dehydrated. Then he runs a few tests and decides it's either salmonella or E. coli. I tell him I don't eat eggs, and he laughs and asks me what the hygiene's like where I'm living and I laugh and tell him I'm living in a shithole, with rodents roaming the kitchen worktop. He explains all about something called pheromones and we decide it's the rats –

FI FI. Mice.

MARNIE (*to* FI FI). Same thing.

(*To audience*.) What done it. The nurse suggests I stay in hospital for a while to recover, but Fi Fi's convinced me to send Autumn to the playscheme with the older kids. She tries to broach a conversation about Autumn going into care temporarily because she can't stay at Merrygold House alone.

FI FI. It's against policy.

MARNIE (*to* FI FI). Damien did.

FI FI. Damien's in Year 7.

MARNIE. I know, I'm just pointing out it's against policy.

FI FI. You could probably do with the respite.

MARNIE. Oh have a day off.

(*To audience*.) My brain feels like it's gonna explode under the pressure. Things can't get no worse. I pull the cannula out and discharge myself when my prayer is finally answered.

SECURITY. I have Liam Dwyer on the line, are you happy for me to connect you?

LIAM. I've been nicked, Marnie, can you send me some money?

MARNIE (*to* LIAM). Who is it?

LIAM. It's Liam, who d'you think it fucking is?

MARNIE. Nah sorry, don't know no Liam.

(*To audience*.) Fi Fi's at the chocolate machine.

(*To* FI FI.) Can I have a word?

FI FI. What have you done now, Marnie?

MARNIE. I reckon I can go home.

FI FI. Are you insane?

MARNIE. *It is safe*. He's in prison.

FI FI. Stephen's in prison?

MARNIE. The thing is. I ain't running from Stevie.

FI FI. Stephen isn't the perpetrator? But we've – Oh I get it. Why are covering for him, Marnie?

MARNIE. Look, I'm grateful for everything and that –

FI FI. What's his name? What's his name? If he exists, what's his name?

MARNIE. I ain't saying.

FI FI. Why not?

MARNIE. Cos I don't need the drama. You're gonna try and take him to court or something and I ain't getting roped in to it.

FI FI. You're still in love with him. You are – aren't you? I can see it in your face.

MARNIE. I'm not.

FI FI. Why are you protecting him? Huh? You clearly don't want him to be punished.

MARNIE. I just wanna go home.

FI FI. Well I'm going to have to discuss my concerns with the family support worker.

MARNIE. Oh fucking hell, forget it. Just forget it. It ain't worth the grief.

(*To audience*.) September the 25th. I'm on the mend –

AUTUMN. Woo-hoo!

MARNIE. And my benefits have finally arrived –

AUTUMN. Woo-hoo!

MARNIE. And Autumn and me are celebrating with a day out at the zoo. We traipse round for a few hours, waving at the animals. It starts to rain so we queue up for the butterfly zone. We're in the line when a beautiful blue-and-white butterfly comes fluttering by.

AUTUMN. Butterfly!

MARNIE. Says Autumn, and she makes a grab for it, splatting it across her arm. The butterfly falls to the ground, dead, except for a twitching wing. A red-faced posh fella points out it was an –

RED-FACED POSH FELLA. Endangered species, for Christ's sake!

MARNIE. The visitors get angry and Autumn starts crying and I tell everyone to go fuck 'emselves, it could have been any kid. And it really could've been any kid! But it was bound to be mine. Let's face it. Chaos follows us everywhere.

It's dusk by the time we get back to Merrygold House. We go straight up to our bedroom and Autumn strips off to get into her pyjamas. We perch on the edge of the bed and she gives me a cuddle, I've forgotten what cuddles feel like.

And then she does. She does something. Something really off-key.

Off-key. And out of character.

(*To* AUTUMN.) That's not funny – (*To audience*.) I say.

(*To* AUTUMN.) That's not funny, stop it. Don't do that, don't do that, stop it, I said. Why are you doing that? Who showed you that? That's rude. That's really rude. That's… private. Why did you just do that, Autumn? Answer me. Why did you do that? What's wrong with you? What's the matter? Tell me, for fuck's sake! Well answer me. Tell me. Tell me who showed you that?

(*To audience*.) I'm tryna work out what I've just witnessed. We stare at each other. She looks petrified.

(*To* AUTUMN.) I wish we could go to the zoo every day –

(*To audience*.) I say – *you know, to try and calm the situation* –

(*To* AUTUMN.) I had a really nice day. It's great spending time together. Talking. You know, talking about stuff. It makes me really happy that we can talk to each other, cos, you know, then I know that you feel like you can trust me. Do you feel like you can trust me? Do you? Can you trust me? So if there's anything you wanna tell me, anything you need to get off your chest. You know.

WHY ARE YOU FUCKING IGNORING ME? HELLO?!

Autumn, this is really important. It's really important that you tell me the truth. Did? If a grown-up… showed you that. I need you to tell me. And you won't be in any trouble. You haven't done anything wrong. But. See the thing is. The thing is. I need to know. If they did. Did a grown-up teach you that?

AUTUMN. Is he a grown-up?

MARNIE (*to audience*). She says.

(*To* AUTUMN.) Who?

AUTUMN. Damien.

MARNIE (*to audience*). You know the feeling when you're asleep in the night and that shadowy Grim Reaper figure appears and pins you to the bed and you're screaming and no sound comes out.

She talks and talks and she's waiting for a response and I can't bring myself to say... anything.

Then she goes –

AUTUMN. Sorry, Mummy.

MARNIE. And she starts to sob.

AUTUMN. I'm sorry, Mummy. I'm – (*Hyperventilating, through tears.*) I'm, I'm sorry, Mummy.

MARNIE. Her little throat gulping. I think back to all the weird conversations Veronica's stuck on me. Late-night knocks on my door, riddle-speaking, tears, abstract confessions and apologies that never made no sense.

I take the chopping knife from the kitchen, for safekeeping. And it's all starting to add up. She clocked this before me. She knew. She protected him.

I phone Fi Fi, on the out-of-hours number, it's loud, she's in a disco, pissed.

FI FI. Don't do anything stupid, Marnie.

MARNIE. She says she'll be in the next morning at –

FI FI. Nine o'clock. There'll be a thorough investigation.

MARNIE. The phone goes dead.

Autumn nods off. Switch the light out.

Stage lights go out, then slowly come back up as night turns into morning.

I sit. I sit on the end of the bed. With the lights out. Thinking. Waiting. For nine o'clock. Waiting. Weeping. Torturing myself. An alarm goes off somewhere. Start to make out voices.

Check my phone. It's seven o'clock. Move towards the door, put my ear to it. Veronica and Damien in the bathroom, talking. Feel sick. I could do it now, couldn't I. Before they suspect anything.

And then Autumn wakes up.

Lock the door. Feel safer, more in control. Of myself. And I pace and I sit and I pace some more and I inspect the kitchen knife with my back turned. So that Autumn can't see. I don't wanna scare her. I'm already scaring her. She's watching me from the bed. Her eyes tell me I'm being weird. And I feel weird. And I don't care. I don't care. I can hear the blood pulsing above my ears, distant noises loud as anything, rigid on the outside, shaking on the inside, high on adrenalin and someone's gonna fucking die. That's my fucking child.

Nine o'clock comes and goes and I'm on the phone to Fi Fi's answer machine and I'm at the window, eyes studying the street. An hour passes and I see her strolling up the road.

She escorts me and Autumn down to the playroom. The hallway's cluttered with staff I've never met, loitering about, eyes darting, whispering to each other. I need a whiskey. I need a whiskey but I settle for a green tea.

I write a statement. No I don't. Fi Fi wants to write it. Start from the beginning. Everything Autumn told me. As thorough, as precise as I can be. Takes the best part of three hours. Fi Fi's got a question for everything: where was I stood when she revealed this part, can I act out that motion –

FI FI. Point, point to where she was touching, show me the object she used –

MARNIE. What makes me say 'rubbing'?

FI FI. Would you mind repeating that again for me?

MARNIE. And I'm done in. I haven't slept in forty-eight hours. I'm filthy with sweat and mascara. I feel mental. If I knew the plot to start with, I definitely don't now.

When we're done Fi Fi says I have –

FI FI. Such a good memory to remember all of that, word for word.

MARNIE. And there's something about the tone that's a bit. I dunno. My spider senses start twitching. I begin to wonder where Fi Fi's motives lie. I mean you don't have to stretch the imagination far to wonder if she's considered how best to extricate herself from a negligence claim.

FI FI. Autumn's very young.

MARNIE (*to* FI FI). She's four –

FI FI. Can I finish? Children of Autumn's age, have vivid imaginations.

MARNIE (*to audience*). I reach for the statement, Fi Fi snatches it up.

FI FI. I'll go and type this up. It needs to be paraphrased.

MARNIE (*to* FI FI). Right, well, I want a photocopy of the original.

FI FI. Well. I'll. Erm. I'll have to check with my supervisor, whether that's allowed.

MARNIE. Why wouldn't it be?

FI FI. Well there's names in it –

MARNIE. Yeah, names that I wrote.

FI FI. I wrote it.

MARNIE. You what?

FI FI. I erm. I just mean, technically I wrote it.

Silence.

MARNIE. I need to go and pack.

FI FI. Marnie, come on! Think about what you're doing. Think about Autumn.

MARNIE. She's safer at home then she was here.

FI FI. Don't defend him, Marnie –

MARNIE. I'M NOT FUCKING DEFENDING THE PRICK!

FI FI. Abuse is abuse –

MARNIE. That's what I thought.

> Can I ask you something, Fi Fi? Can I? Has Damien done anything like this before?

> *Beat.*

> Has he?

> *Beat.*

FI FI. All our clients' files are confidential.

MARNIE. Did you know he was a risk?

> *Sound effect – door slamming.*

> (*To audience.*) Veronica's back.

FI FI. There's a space, at our sister refuge. You can go today. Now if you like. I hear your concerns but. There's some really lovely children there, younger children, with *less behavioural problems*.

MARNIE (*to* FI FI). No thanks. We're going home.

FI FI. You can't go home.

MARNIE. I can go where I want.

FI FI. Yes but you can't take Autumn with you. No one will authorise that.

MARNIE (*to audience*). We've accumulated too much to take in one go. Fi Fi won't allow us to come back for the rest. So we make two piles, stuff to take and stuff to bin. Emma arrives early for her shift.

EMMA. Would you like a sweet, Autumn?

MARNIE. Emma helps me pack.

EMMA. If you *are* going to go to the police, go tonight, don't leave it, you won't have a leg to stand on. And don't leave here without that statement.

MARNIE (*to* EMMA). D'you believe me?

EMMA. Absolutely.

MARNIE (*to audience*). Fi Fi's back.

(*To* FI FI). Have you got my statement, Fi Fi?

FI FI. Yeah, I've just asked about that, Marnie... and... I'm really sorry but we're not permitted to give you a copy. For confidentiality purposes.

MARNIE (*to* FI FI). Right.

FI FI. I'm really sorry –

MARNIE. Yeah we've established that, Fi Fi – where does that leave us?

Silence.

(*To audience.*) I let out a laugh. I mean, you'd have to be pretty fucking stupid to believe Fi Fi would risk her neck to stick up for a child. That sort of thing takes character.

FI FI. Not to be pushy, Marnie, but I clock off in five minutes –

MARNIE (*to* FI FI). I ain't leaving without that statement. You're gonna have to drag me out of here.

FI FI. But. Well the police'll have to be called –

MARNIE. Ring them. Ring them. By all means, please.

FI FI. We don't want to have to do that, Marnie –

MARNIE. No I bet you don't. I bet you don't. Well in that case, I advise you to go downstairs and talk to your *supervisor* again, see if you can work something out, cos I ain't in no rush and like I say, I ain't going nowhere without it.

FI FI. Marnie –

MARNIE. GO AND GET ME THE PAPER, FI FI, GO AND GET ME THE PAPER, I'M NOT LEAVING WITHOUT THAT STATEMENT, GET ME THAT FUCKING PAPER!!!

(*To audience*.) I get the statement. I mean I have to barricade us in the room for an hour but I get a photocopy of the statement. All the names and half the conversation have been blacked out, it's illegible, but I get it.

VERONICA – *loud wailing*.

Veronica's been informed. She's in the hallway wailing and screaming that I'm evil. She's making more fuss than me.

Bundle into my motor. Can't see out the rearview over the bin liners. We're at a loss for places to crash. It dawns on me to ring Florence. We head to her bedsit out in Dagenham. I mean she ain't the full ticket but fucking beggars can't be choosers.

We're making a bed on Florence's pull-out when the policemen turn up. They talk to Autumn, note down that she's distressed.

MARNIE (*to* YOUNG POLICEMAN). So, what's the next step?

YOUNG POLICEMAN. Social Services should attend first thing – I'd advise you to confirm though, they're usually very busy.

MARNIE (*to audience*). September the 27th. No one attends first thing. Florence gives them a ring.

FLORENCE. Got cut off.

MARNIE (*to* FLORENCE). Call back.

FLORENCE. Rung out.

MARNIE. Try again.

FLORENCE. Answer machine.

MARNIE. Leave a message.

(*To audience*.) We don't hear back. We call back at closing. They ain't coming. Bed down for another night with Florence.

September the 30th. A letter arrives. From a woman called Hillary Nunn. It's short and to the point: a meeting's been held and based on the information put forth the case has been

closed without investigation. Wait till Monday, ring Hillary.
(*To* HILLARY.) Why would you hold a meeting without me
there? What d'you mean I had the opportunity to attend, no
one invited me... Well you ain't even spoke to her yet...
What d'you mean there's not enough information? There's
other kids corroborating her story... That's the point of an
investigation!

(*To audience*.) Apparently 'someone' at this meeting, alleges
that there's –

FI FI. Reason to believe –

MARNIE. That the only reason we've left Merrygold House is
to –

FI FI. Return to the perpetrator –

MARNIE. Who this 'someone' happens to know is called –

FI FI. Stephen Gallagher.

MARNIE. So it's left to Merrygold House – to investigate
Merrygold House. Which sounds absolutely fucking
diabolical to me, given the accusations I'm brandishing, but
what the fuck do I know?

October the 3rd. The police've dropped my harassment
charges. No thanks to that turncoat, Fi Fi. I should be feeling
jammy right now. Cos they're threatening to do Stevie's bird
for perjury. I ain't though. I'm struggling to feel at all.

October the 9th. Still ain't had a visit from Social Services.
We can't exactly stay here. It's good of Florence, but I mean,
she's... you know. Not well. And there's a lot at stake here.
I keep putting forth the case for us to go home. I explain it's
safe an' that. That the 'perpetrator', for want of another
word, that he's in prison. But Hillary Nunn – the voice at the
end of a phone – she ain't prepared to take my word for it.
Hillary says there'll be repercussions if I take Autumn back
to my flat, but she can't offer housing solutions. We can't do
much else but stay put. But it leaves the pair of us in limbo.
Autumn's not going to school. I can't go back to work.

We drive over to the council offices to get some housing advice. The doors are closing when we arrive and the old bint behind the counter wants to go home. Silvia, her name is. Tells me to make it quick. I rush through some backstory but it's obvious Silvia ain't keeping up.

SILVIA. You won't get a house just like that. You'll have to join the list, like everyone else.

MARNIE. I explain I've already got a tenancy – Silvia interjects –

SILVIA. Well then you need to go home.

MARNIE. I run over the story again, cos Silvia ain't quite grasping the predicament –

(*To* SILVIA.) We've come from a refuge – (*To audience*.) I say.

SILVIA. Well then you need to go back there.

MARNIE (*to* SILVIA). *We ain't going back* because everything what I've just told you, are you listening to me, Silvia, or what?

(*To audience*.) Silvia says I've made us intentionally homeless, that the council don't have a duty to house us. I can't even be fucked to row with her.

Back to Florence's for a second police visit. Give Florence a tenner and point her towards the pub, before anyone has an opportunity to pick holes in her. Autumn crawls behind the couch. The coppers wanna question her alone, but she hides out till they give up tryna coax her. They question me instead. What sort of character am I? They wanna know whether Fi Fi would agree with this testimonial of me. Trick question, I reckon. Pretty sure they would of spoke to her already.

OLD POLICEMAN. Right. So. Right. Let me try and get this straight, because it's a little bit. Confusing. To say the least. The person you are fleeing. Who held you against your will, and, and, and –

MARNIE (*to* OLD POLICEMAN). Strangled me and that
yeah –

OLD POLICEMAN. That's right, who hit you –

MARNIE. Yeah hit me and that. I mean it makes it sound not
that bad, like he give me a slap or something, when you say
'hit'. It was actually bad. Like I left my home and stuff. Well
he was, you know.

OLD POLICEMAN. Yes we've got that part. This person – *who
you're refusing to name* – you're saying he's not *Mr
Gallagher*, who made the allegations of harassment against –

MARNIE. False allegations, they were false. They got dropped.

OLD POLICEMAN. Why won't you give us his name?

MARNIE (*to audience*). Alex, with the eyes – you remember –
she got cornered into going to court. A lot of upset for
nothing – first she was called a liar, then the case got
dropped and now the ex is looking to bury her – I've got
enough problems.

OLD POLICEMAN. You'd be protected.

MARNIE (*to* OLD POLICEMAN). Not being funny and that.
But you can't protect us from him. I rang you. I've rung you
in the past.

OLD POLICEMAN. He can't harm you if he's in prison.

MARNIE. They can't lock him up forever. He'll get out. And
then he'll kill me.

OLD POLICEMAN. So. Getting back to the, you know. Neither
of those two people are the child's father?

MARNIE. No. No her dad's alright actually.

OLD POLICEMAN. And where is the father?

MARNIE. He's in prison.

OLD POLICEMAN. And there's nothing you've failed to tell
us. No skeletons in the closet?

MARNIE (*to audience*). The old boy wants to know.

(*To* OLD POLICEMAN.) Skeletons?

OLD POLICEMAN. You know, skeletons. Like, pffft –

FI FI. Mental-health issues –

MARNIE. Mental-health issues?

OLD POLICEMAN. Yes.

MARNIE. Well… yeah… sort of. I get depressed and stuff. And you know, anxious. I ain't *mental-mental*.

(*To audience*.) It's a bit of a sticking point with them. As though this has some bearing on my credibility.

(*To* OLD POLICEMAN.) Shouldn't you. Sorry. It's just. I was hoping you'd investigate my daughter's disclosure? Only it feels like you're investigating me.

OLD POLICEMAN. Look. It's not really suitable, this place, is it. A bedsit. For a child, I mean. She needs a settled environment –

MARNIE. Florence ain't on her feet yet.

OLD POLICEMAN. And how long have you known this Florence –

MARNIE. I dunno. Three, four months.

OLD POLICEMAN. Is she? You know. The full shilling?

MARNIE. Well I don't see why we shouldn't stay with her for a while – we've already shared a home with her – at Merrygold House – she weren't considered dangerous then.

OLD POLICEMAN. We still need to look at what's best for the child.

MARNIE. What's best for the child is a full investigation, some bloody counselling, don't you think?

OLD POLICEMAN. And in the meantime, where is she going to live?

MARNIE. I'll have to find somewhere, won't I – we've got our own bloody flat!

OLD POLICEMAN. Has the social worker discussed signing Autumn into temporary care?

MARNIE. We haven't had a social worker visit.

OLD POLICEMAN. Are you familiar with how it works?

MARNIE. No one's taking my kid!

OLD POLICEMAN. It would only be a temporary measure.

MARNIE. Not happening –

OLD POLICEMAN. You can remove her at any given time.

MARNIE. Yeah *course* I can. Until someone sits me down to break the news she's been forced adopted.

OLD POLICEMAN. It's not really in our hands, you see.

MARNIE. I'm not doing it. Look at me, look at me. I ain't doing it.

(*To audience.*) Florence and me sit up till the small hours drinking tea and crying.

FLORENCE. We'll go to the papers. Or, or bigger – we'll petition the Government.

MARNIE (*to* FLORENCE). Florence, you're a recluse –

FLORENCE. They're not gonna silence us. Leave it with me.

MARNIE (*to audience*). You know your life's gone to pot when your only mate in the world's a teetotal convicted arsonist.

I can see the future. Really clearly. There's only me and Florence in it.

I'm thinking of putting a rope round my neck.

When Florence finally goes to bed, I lie down on the couch, take out my phone and I google 'death by asphyxiation'.

I just feel *really* sad.

Lights fade to blackout.

Lights come up. MARNIE *engages in play with* AUTUMN.

JOANNE. Miss McCabe? Miss McCabe. We're ready for you.

MARNIE (*to* JOANNE). I'm not doing it.

JOANNE. It's your choice.

MARNIE. How have I got any choice in this? Explain that to me.

JOANNE. You can either –

MARNIE. Sign my child away, or you're gonna –

JOANNE. Make an application to the courts –

MARNIE. Take her anyway –

JOANNE. For a care order.

MARNIE. That ain't choice.

JOANNE. Miss McCabe.

MARNIE. I already told you – the fella's banged up!

JOANNE. We need to know you're cooperating with us.

MARNIE. You're going on like I'd put her in danger.

JOANNE. We need to establish some trust.

MARNIE. All I want. All I'm asking for is an investigation. And it's like. It feels like, you're all too busy shining the spotlight back at me.

JOANNE. I'm interested in the truth.

MARNIE. I've give you the truth.

JOANNE (*sighs*). What's his name?

Silence.

What's his name? This '*fella*'?

Silence.

MARNIE. If I tell you his name, will it put an end to this? Can we focus on the matter at hand then?

Silence.

Yeah or No?

JOANNE. Yes.

Silence.

MARNIE. Liam Dwyer.

Silence. JOANNE *is thinking.*

JOANNE. Has Stephen told you to say this?

MARNIE *exhales.*

I need the truth, Marnie.

MARNIE. You're *deaf* to the truth.

JOANNE. Are you and Stephen in contact?

MARNIE. No. I haven't spoke to neither of them.

JOANNE. And you're sure of that?

MARNIE. Are you hard of hearing? D'you usually base your evidence on hearsay? It's just I thought you was s'posed to examine the facts, before you draw conclusions and that.

Look. Joanna –

JOANNE. It's Joanne.

MARNIE. Same thing. Listen. Joanne. We've got a flat. We've actually got a fucking home. It might not of crossed your mind, but that – (*Signals to* AUTUMN.) ain't a number on a piece of paper, for me, to tick off throughout the working day. That's my fucking child. If I thought she was in danger I'd tell you my fucking self. She's fed, she's clean, she's well-rounded, given what happened – you agree. I don't wallop her, I don't belittle her, I don't leave her with Tom, Dick and Harry. I ain't a bad mum. I'm not here because I'll put her in harm's way. Or, or, because you say I might pose a *future* risk of emotional harm. All I've done is stand up for my child.

Let me take her home.

JOANNE. Autumn's safety comes first –

MARNIE. Well then find us somewhere to live!

JOANNE. Me?

MARNIE. Yeah, you, Joanne. You – the one who's paid to deal with this shit.

JOANNE. As you've already been told – on numerous occasions – Social Services, don't have the power to do that. We don't have the resources!

MARNIE. But you can afford to put her through the care system? That must cost a few quid.

What am I s'posed to do? Tell me… you tell me cos I don't know any more. What do I do? What do I do?

Lighting shift to signify change in scene.

The actor – or actors – provoke a dialogue with the audience.

nabokov.

producer@nabokov-online.com

nabokov create theatre that immediately responds to the world around us, reflecting the diverse experiences and stories of our time. Their mission is to ensure that theatre is inclusive and accessible for all. The company has a bold artistic vision to champion diverse voices to reach new audiences with new theatrical forms that reflect their experiences.

nabokov has a fifteen-year history of discovering, developing and producing new talent and creating award-winning productions and distinctive theatrical events. They believe that theatre should come to audiences and be performed in community spaces from car parks and the streets to rooms above pubs and not just restricted to traditional spaces. They aim to nurture new talent, represent the working-class female voice and engage new audiences by authentically representing their experiences.

@nabokovtheatre
www.facebook.com/nabokovtheatre
www.nabokov-online.com

THE
MARLOWE

Creating experiences that enrich, inspire and entertain

The Marlowe is one of the country's most successful regional theatres, bringing the work of prestigious companies such as the National, Royal Shakespeare Company, Matthew Bourne and Glyndebourne Opera to audiences in Kent. The Marlowe are committed to nurturing and inspiring creative talent with new writing at the heart of what they do.

Roar, The Marlowe's new-writing development programme, works to support emerging writers and artists by providing the opportunity to develop bold and exciting new work through mentoring, workshops, funded research and development and work-in-progress sharings.

Since reopening in 2011, The Marlowe has been committed to championing new writing and to date have been involved in the realisation of a number of productions including: *Beached* by Melissa Bubnic, which premiered at The Marlowe Studio in 2014 before transferring to Soho Theatre, London. This was followed by *A Better Woman* by Simon Mendes da Costa in 2015. The Marlowe have also co-produced a number of new-writing productions, most recently: *Run The Beast Down* by Titas Halder, which premiered at The Marlowe Studio before transferring to Finborough Theatre, London in January 2017, *Warrior Poets* which was developed in collaboration with Wise Words Festival and directed by Lemn Sissay which premiered at The Marlowe Studio in October 2016. The Marlowe are associate producers on *Kanye The First* by Sam Steiner which premieres at HighTide Festival in September 2017. Other productions include *Mobile* with The Paper Birds Theatre Company and Edinburgh First Award-winning *Fabric* in association with Robin Rayner and TREMers.

The Friars, Canterbury, CT1 2AS
info@marlowetheatre.com
marlowetheatre.com

This production has been made possible with the support of The Marlowe Theatre Development Trust. Registered Charity no 1120751

www.nickhernbooks.co.uk

facebook.com/nickhernbooks

twitter.com/nickhernbooks